Mama Hen, Come Quick!

Written by Janet Fisher   Illustrated by Yuri Salzman

Mama Hen, come quick.

Your little chick is sick!

3

Mama Cat, come quick.

4

Your little kitten is sick!

5

Mama Bear, come quick.

6

Your little cub is sick!

They are not sick.

It was a trick!